THIRD EDITION

WORKBOOK

Grasping God's Word

THIRD EDITION

WORKBOOK

Grasping God's Word

A Hands-On Approach to
Reading, Interpreting,
and Applying the Bible

J. Scott Duvall
J. Daniel Hays

ZONDERVAN®

ZONDERVAN.com/
AUTHORTRACKER
follow your favorite authors

ZONDERVAN

Grasping God's Word Workbook
Copyright © 2001, 2005, 2012 by J. Scott Duvall and J. Daniel Hays

Requests for information should be addressed to:

Zondervan, *Grand Rapids, Michigan 49530*

ISBN 978-0-310-49259-7

Cover design: Rob Monacelli
Cover photography: Getty Images
Interior design: Sherri L. Hoffman

Printed in the United States of America

13 14 15 16 17 /PHP/ 26 25 24 23 22 21 20 19 18 17 16 15 14 13 12 11 10 9 8 7 6 5 4 3

CONTENTS

INTRODUCTION

Welcome to the workbook for *Grasping God's Word*. This workbook is designed to be used in close conjunction with the main textbook. It is comprised of two main sections. Section 1 contains tear-out assignment sheets that pertain to each chapter of the textbook. The students will complete these assignments and hand them in as they finish each chapter, according to the instructor's schedule. For most chapters, the workbook contains numerous assignments, usually more than is feasible for the student to complete as homework. These extra assignments can be used for in-class examples or for in-class group work. Section 2 relates to writing an exegetical paper. This section contains guidelines for writing the paper, a list of suggested texts in Ephesians, and tear-out sheets for each of the texts from Ephesians.

Note that there are several assignments included in section 1 that relate to the exegetical paper, allowing the students to work on various aspects of their respective passages throughout the semester. For example, in chapter 4 the students' regular assignments consist of making observations on various biblical passages. Those classes that include the exegetical paper as part of the class requirements should have the students complete assignment 6 of that chapter. In this exercise the instructor first assigns the student one of the passages from the list of Ephesian texts in assignment 6. The student then makes observations on his or her particular assigned passage. The tear-out sheets for these texts can be found in section 2. The student also completes the corresponding assignments for the exegetical paper in chapter 6 ("Historical-Cultural Context"), chapter 8 ("Literary Context"), and chapter 9 ("Word Studies").

The assignments that relate to the exegetical paper are marked in the workbook with the heading "Exegetical Paper." They include: chapter 4—assignment 6; chapter 6—assignment 6; chapter 8—assignment 3; and chapter 9—assignment 6. Thus by the end of the semester, when the exegetical paper is due, the students will have already completed four assignments dealing with various aspects of their passage.

ASSIGNMENT WORKSHEETS

PART 1

How to Read the Book — Basic Tools

BIBLE TRANSLATIONS Chapter 1

NAME   DATE

Assignment 1-1

Select five translations that we talked about in this chapter. Select a passage from the Bible (it must be at least two verses long) and write out how these translations render this passage. Next, mark or highlight the differences among the five translations. Write a paragraph summarizing what you have observed by comparing the translations.

Assignment 1 – 2

Answer the following questions:

1. Do you agree that the Bible is a divine-human book? Why or why not?

2. What is textual criticism? How is it possible to have a high view of the authority of the Bible and a positive view of textual criticism at the same time?

3. What is a Bible translation? Why is translation not a simple exercise? Describe the two main approaches to translation discussed in this chapter. Which approach do you feel most comfortable with? Why?

THE INTERPRETIVE JOURNEY Chapter 2

NAME _____ DATE _____

Assignment 2-1

Describe the five steps of the Interpretive Journey.

Step 1:

Step 2:

Step 3:

Step 4:

Step 5:

Assignment 2-2

What are the guidelines for developing theological principles?

1.

2.

3.

4.

5.

Assignment 2-3

What are the differences that determine the width of the river to cross?

HOW TO READ THE BOOK—SENTENCES   Chapter 3

NAME _____   DATE _____

Assignment 3-1

Find a *minimum* of thirty observations in Acts 1:8. List them below. Avoid making interpretations or applications at this stage. That is, stay with observations. For example, an observation would be to note that the passage starts off with the conjunction "but." This conjunction connects the sentence to the one above it in a contrasting way. If, however, you were to note that the Holy Spirit empowers us for evangelism, that observation falls into the category of interpretation or application. Do not enter the interpretation or application phase yet. Limit all thirty of your observations to the details and not to the interpretation of the details. Work hard! Dig deep! Read and reread the passage. Do not quit until you have found at least thirty observations. Try to find more than thirty. Happy hunting!

But you will receive power when the Holy Spirit comes on you;

and you will be my witnesses in Jerusalem,

and in all Judea and Samaria,

and to the ends of the earth.

1.

2.

3.

4.

5.

6.

7.

8.

9.

10.

11.

12.

13.

14.

15.

16.

17.

18.

19.

20.

21.

22.

23.

24.

25.

26.

27.

28.

29.

30.

Extra 1.

Extra 2.

Extra 3.

Extra 4.

Use another sheet of paper if you have more.

Assignment 3-2

Make as many observations as you can on 1 John 1:5–7. Follow the format presented for Romans 12:1–2 in chapter 3 of the textbook. Dig deep! Think hard. Spend time on this. Mark dozens and dozens of observations. Read and reread. Look again. Observe! Observe! Observe!

[5]This is the message that we have heard from him

and declare to you: God is light;

in him there is no darkness at all.

[6]If we claim to have fellowship with him

and yet walk in the darkness, we lie and do not live out the truth.

[7]But if we walk in the light, as he is in the light,

we have fellowship with one another,

and the blood of Jesus, his Son, purifies us from all sin.

Assignment 3-3

Make as many observations as you can on Deuteronomy 6:4–6. Follow the format presented for Romans 12:1–2 in chapter 3 of the textbook.

[4]Hear, O Israel: The LORD our God, the LORD is one.

[5]Love the LORD your God with all your heart

and with all your soul and with all your strength.

[6]These commandments that I give you today

are to be on your hearts.

Assignment 3-4

Make as many observations as you can on 1 Timothy 6:17–19. Follow the format presented for Romans 12:1–2 in chapter 3 of the textbook.

[17]Command those who are rich in this present world

not to be arrogant nor to put their hope in wealth,

which is so uncertain, but to put their hope in God,

who richly provides us with everything for our enjoyment.

[18]Command them to do good, to be rich in good deeds,

and to be generous and willing to share.

[19]In this way they will lay up treasure for themselves

as a firm foundation for the coming age,

so that they may take hold of the life that is truly life.

Assignment 3-5

Make as many observations as you can on Matthew 28:18–20. Follow the format presented for Romans 12:1–2 in chapter 3 of the textbook.

[18]Then Jesus came to them and said,

"All authority in heaven and on earth

has been given to me.

[19]Therefore go and make disciples of all nations,

baptizing them in the name of the Father

and of the Son and of the Holy Spirit,

[20]and teaching them to obey

everything I have commanded you.

And surely I am with you always,

to the very end of the age."

HOW TO READ THE BOOK—PARAGRAPHS   Chapter 4

NAME _____   DATE _____

Assignment 4-1

Try making observations on Philippians 2:1–4. Write down as many observations as you can. Write in the text and in the margins.

¹Therefore if you have any encouragement from being united with Christ,

if any comfort from his love,

if any common sharing in the Spirit,

if any tenderness and compassion,

²then make my joy complete by being like-minded,

having the same love, being one in spirit and of one mind.

³Do nothing out of selfish ambition or vain conceit,

Rather, in humility value others above yourselves,

not looking to your own interests

but each of you to the interests of the others.

Assignment 4-2

Make as many observations as you can on 1 Corinthians 1:18–25. Dig deep! Think hard. This is not an easy passage. Spend time on this. Mark dozens and dozens of observations. Read and reread. Look again. Observe! Observe! Observe!

[18]For the message of the cross is foolishness to those who are

perishing, but to us who are being saved it is the power of God.

[19]For it is written:

"I will destroy the wisdom of the wise;

the intelligence of the intelligent I will frustrate."

[20]Where is the wise person? Where is the teacher of the law?

Where is the philosopher of this age?

Has not God made foolish the wisdom of the world?

[21]For since in the wisdom of God the world

through its wisdom did not know him,

God was pleased through the foolishness of what was preached

to save those who believe.

[22]Jews demand signs and Greeks look for wisdom,

[23]but we preach Christ crucified:

a stumbling block to Jews and foolishness to Gentiles,

[24]but to those whom God has called, both Jews and Greeks,

Christ the power of God and the wisdom of God.

[25]For the foolishness of God is wiser than human wisdom,

and the weakness of God is stronger than human strength.

Assignment 4-3

Make as many observations as you can on Colossians 3:1–4. Dig deep! Think hard. Spend time on this. Mark dozens and dozens of observations. Read and reread! Look again! Observe! Observe! Observe!

[1]Since, then, you have been raised with Christ,

set your hearts on things above,

where Christ is, seated at the right hand of God.

[2]Set your minds on things above,

not on earthly things.

[3]For you died, and your life is now hidden with Christ in God.

[4]When Christ, who is your life, appears,

then you also will appear with him in glory.

Assignment 4-4

Make as many observations as you can on Psalm 1:1–3. Dig deep! Think hard. Spend time on this. Mark dozens and dozens of observations. Read and reread! Look again! Observe! Observe! Observe!

[1]Blessed is the one

who does not walk in step with the wicked

or stand in the way that sinners take

or sit in the company of mockers,

[2]but whose delight is in the law of the Lord,

and who meditates on his law day and night.

[3]That person is like a tree planted by streams of water,

which yields its fruit in season

and whose leaf does not wither—

whatever they do prospers.

Assignment 4-5

Make as many observations as you can on Matthew 6:25–34. Dig deep! Think hard. Spend time on this. Mark dozens and dozens of observations. Read and reread! Look again! Observe! Observe! Observe!

25"Therefore I tell you, do not worry about your life, what you

will eat or drink; or about your body, what you will wear.

Is not life more important than food, and the body more that clothes?

26Look at the birds of the air; they do not sow or reap or

store away in barns, and yet your heavenly Father feeds them.

Are you not much more valuable than they?

27Can any one of you by worrying add a single hour to your life?

28And why do you worry about clothes?

See how the flowers of the field grow. They do not labor or spin.

29Yet I tell you that not even Solomon in all his splendor was

dressed like one of these.

30If that is how God clothes the grass of the field,

which is here today and tomorrow is thrown into the fire,

will he not much more clothe you—you of little faith?

31So do not worry, saying, 'What shall we eat?' or

'What shall we drink?' or 'What shall we wear?'

32For the pagans run after all these things,

and your heavenly Father knows that you need them.

[33]But seek first his kingdom and his righteousness,

and all these things will be given to you as well.

[34]Therefore do not worry about tomorrow,

for tomorrow will worry about itself.

Each day has enough trouble of its own.

Assignment 4-6 (Exegetical Paper)

Your professor will assign you one of the passages from Ephesians listed below. Find that passage in section 2 at the end of this workbook. Make as many observations on that passage as you can and hand in that sheet with your observations marked on it. Dig deep! Think hard! Look again! Observe! Observe! Observe!

☐ Ephesians 1:3–6
☐ Ephesians 1:7–10
☐ Ephesians 1:11–14
☐ Ephesians 1:15–23
☐ Ephesians 2:1–7
☐ Ephesians 2:8–13
☐ Ephesians 2:14–22
☐ Ephesians 3:1–7
☐ Ephesians 3:8–13
☐ Ephesians 3:14–21
☐ Ephesians 4:1–6

☐ Ephesians 4:11–16
☐ Ephesians 4:17–24
☐ Ephesians 4:25–32
☐ Ephesians 5:1–6
☐ Ephesians 5:7–14
☐ Ephesians 5:15–21
☐ Ephesians 5:22–33
☐ Ephesians 6:1–9
☐ Ephesians 6:10–16
☐ Ephesians 6:17–20

HOW TO READ THE BOOK—DISCOURSES Chapter 5

NAME _____   DATE _____

Assignment 5-1

Make as many observations as you can on Nehemiah 1:1–11.

¹The words of Nehemiah son of Hakaliah: In the month of Kislev

in the twentieth year, while I was in the citadel of Susa,

²Hanani, one of my brothers, came from Judah with some other men,

and I questioned them about the Jewish remnant

that had survived the exile, and also about Jerusalem.

³They said to me, "Those who survived the exile and are back

in the province are in great trouble and disgrace. The wall of

Jerusalem is broken down, and its gates have been burned with fire."

⁴When I heard these things, I sat down and wept. For some days

I mourned and fasted and prayed before the God of heaven.

⁵Then I said: "Lord, the God of heaven, the great and awesome God,

who keeps his covenant of love with those who love him and keep

his commandments,

⁶let your ear be attentive and your eyes open to hear the prayer

your servant is praying before you day and night for your servants,

the people of Israel. I confess the sins we Israelites, including

myself and my father's family, have committed against you.

[7]We have acted very wickedly toward you. We have not obeyed the

commands, decrees and laws you gave your servant Moses.

[8]Remember the instruction you gave your servant Moses, saying,

'If you are unfaithful, I will scatter you among the nations,

[9]but if you return to me and obey my commands,

then even if your exiled people are at the farthest horizon,

I will gather them from there and bring them to the place

I have chosen as a dwelling for my Name.'

[10]They are your servants and your people,

whom you redeemed by your great strength and your mighty hand.

[11]Lord, let your ear be attentive to the prayer of this your servant

and to the prayer of your servants who delight in revering your

name. Give your servant success today by granting him favor in the

presence of this man." I was cupbearer to the king.

Assignment 5-2

Read the story below from Mark 5:21–43. Actually it is two stories. The first story is about Jairus and his daughter. The second story is about a bleeding woman. Note that the second story interrupts the first; that is, the bleeding-woman story is presented right in the middle of the Jairus episode. This is suggestive to us. Look at the two stories and list as many direct comparisons and contrasts between the two as you can find. Read carefully! Look hard! There are many to find. Write on the back if you need more space.

[21]When Jesus had again crossed over by boat to the other side of the lake, a large crowd gathered around him while he was by the lake. [22]Then one of the synagogue leaders, named Jairus, came, and when he saw Jesus, he fell at his feet. [23]He pleaded earnestly with him, "My little daughter is dying. Please come and put your hands on her so that she will be healed and live." [24]So Jesus went with him.

A large crowd followed and pressed around him. [25]And a woman was there who had been subject to bleeding for twelve years. [26]She had suffered a great deal under the care of many doctors and had spent all she had, yet instead of getting better she grew worse. [27]When she heard about Jesus, she came up behind him in the crowd and touched his cloak, [28]because she thought, "If I just touch his clothes, I will be healed." [29]Immediately her bleeding stopped and she felt in her body that she was freed from her suffering.

[30]At once Jesus realized that power had gone out from him. He turned around in the crowd and asked, "Who touched my clothes?"

[31]"You see the people crowding against you," his disciples answered, "and yet you can ask, 'Who touched me?'"

[32]But Jesus kept looking around to see who had done it. [33]Then the woman, knowing what had happened to her, came and fell at his feet and, trembling with fear, told him the whole truth. [34]He said to her, "Daughter, your faith has healed you. Go in peace and be freed from your suffering."

[35]While Jesus was still speaking, some people came from the house of Jairus, the synagogue leader. "Your daughter is dead," they said. "Why bother the teacher anymore?"

[36]Overhearing what they said, Jesus told him, "Don't be afraid; just believe."

[37]He did not let anyone follow him except Peter, James and John the brother of James. [38]When they came to the home of the synagogue leader, Jesus saw a commotion, with people crying and wailing loudly. [39]He went in and said to them, "Why all this commotion and wailing? The child is not dead but asleep." [40]But they laughed at him.

After he put them all out, he took the child's father and mother and the disciples who were with him, and went in where the child was. [41]He took her by the hand and said to her, *"Talitha koum!"* (which means, "Little girl, I say to you, get up!"). [42]Immediately the girl stood up and began to walk around (she was twelve years old). At this they were completely astonished. [43]He gave strict orders not to let anyone know about this, and told them to give her something to eat.

Just to get you started:

Jairus	Bleeding Woman
1. a man	1. a woman
2. asks Jesus for help publicly	2. asks Jesus for help privately

continued on reverse side

Jairus	Bleeding Woman

Assignment 5-3

Read the story below from Mark 11 and make as many observations as you can on the text. Notice that the text has two encounters with a fig tree (vv. 12–14, 19–21) sandwiched around an event in the temple (vv. 15–18). In addition to making observations, explain how the fig tree relates to the episode in the temple.

¹²The next day as they were leaving Bethany, Jesus was hungry.

¹³Seeing in the distance a fig tree in leaf, he went to find out if it

had any fruit. When he reached it, he found nothing but leaves,

because it was not the season for figs.

¹⁴Then he said to the tree, "May no one ever eat fruit from you

again." And his disciples heard him say it.

¹⁵On reaching Jerusalem, Jesus entered the temple courts

and began driving out those who were buying and selling there.

He overturned the tables of the money changers and

the benches of those selling doves,

¹⁶and would not allow anyone to carry merchandise

through the temple courts.

¹⁷And as he taught them, he said, "Is it not written:

'My house will be called a house of prayer for all nations'?

But you have made it 'a den of robbers.'"

¹⁸The chief priests and the teachers of the law heard this

and began looking for a way to kill him, for they feared him,

because the whole crowd was amazed at his teaching.

¹⁹When evening came, Jesus and his disciples went out of the city.

[20]In the morning, as they went along, they saw

the fig tree withered from the roots.

[21]Peter remembered and said to Jesus, "Rabbi, look!

The fig tree you cursed has withered!"

Explanation: How does the fig tree incident relate to the episode in the temple?

PART 2

Contexts — Now and Then

THE HISTORICAL-CULTURAL CONTEXT Chapter 6

NAME _____   DATE _____

Assignment 6-1

In the New Testament letter of Philemon, the apostle Paul writes on behalf of a slave named Onesimus. Part of identifying the historical-cultural context of Philemon includes knowing something about the institution of slavery in the Greco-Roman world. Consult several New Testament histories, Bible dictionaries, or Bible encyclopedias and read their articles on slavery. Then write a one- to two-page summary of the practice of slavery in New Testament times. If your professor requires you to type this assignment, then use regular printer paper. Otherwise use both sides of this sheet.

Assignment 6-2

Look up Haggai in an Old Testament survey or introduction and read what the author(s) has to say by way of introduction (e.g., author, date, audience, situation, purpose). Use what you have learned to write a one- to two-page description of the historical setting of this prophetic book. If your professor requires you to type this assignment, then use regular printer paper. Otherwise use both sides of this sheet.

Assignment 6-3

Read Revelation 2–3 and list the seven churches that receive a letter. Next, locate the seven churches (their cities) on the map of Asia Minor supplied on this page. Trace the route among the seven churches that a messenger probably followed to deliver the letter. Finally, look up Revelation 3:14–22 in a commentary or background commentary and make a list of every historical-cultural fact about Laodicea that you can find.

Churches in Revelation 2:1–3:22:

1. Ephesus _____

2. _____

3. _____

4. _____

5. _____

6. _____

7. _____

Write down historical-cultural facts about Laodicea.

Assignment 6-4

Read the conversation between Jesus and the Samaritan woman recorded in John 4:1–39. Then read an article on "Samaria" or "Samaritan" in a Bible dictionary or encyclopedia and make a list of all the ways that the article helps you understand the conversation between Jesus and the woman.

Assignment 6-5

Use a Bible dictionary or encyclopedia to answer the following questions about the book of Nehemiah:

1. How much time passes between the month of Kislev (or Chislev) in Nehemiah 1:1 and the month of Nisan in Nehemiah 2:1?

2. Where is Susa (Neh. 1:1)?

3. For which empire did Susa serve as one of three royal cities?

4. What other biblical character lived in Susa?

5. Did this character live before Nehemiah or after?

6. Which empire did King Artaxerxes rule over and when (Neh. 2:1)?

7. What was a cupbearer's (Neh. 1:11) status in the royal court?

Assignment 6-6 (Exegetical Paper)

The book of Ephesians was probably intended to be circulated and read throughout Asia Minor. The city of Ephesus was the most influential city in this region. Discover as much historical-cultural background information about Ephesus as you can. Write the results of your research in a "report" form. Include the location, the size, the economy, a brief history, the religion, the language, other cultural items of interest, and the role that Ephesus plays in the Bible (especially in the book of Acts). Use extra paper as needed. Type the assignment if your professor requires it.

WHAT DO *WE* BRING TO THE TEXT? Chapter 7

NAME   DATE

Assignment 7-1

In three or four typed pages, describe your family background in regard to cultural influences. Discuss as well as you can both your mother (and her family) and your father (and his family). Include any other families who may have influenced you as well. For each, discuss attitudes and views toward religion, family, work, education, and wealth. Describe the socioeconomic location of your family and its religious context. Also, how do members of your family tend to relate to each other? Does your family tend to be warm and "huggy" or cold and distant? Finally, try to relate your family background to your own set of values and outlooks. What have you retained? What have you rejected?

Note: This assignment is not meant to pry into your personal life. Feel free to omit anything in the written assignment about which you are sensitive. But be sure to *think* about those things you omit so that you are aware of their influence on your study of the Bible. This exercise is a self-analysis; it is for your benefit and not ours.

THE LITERARY CONTEXT Chapter 8

NAME _____ DATE _____

Assignment 8-1

Write a paragraph describing the surrounding context of the following passages:

1. Acts 1:7–8

2. 1 Corinthians 11:27–32

Assignment 8-2

Turn to the Old Testament book of Jonah and do the following:

1. Read the entire book and identify how the book is divided into paragraphs or sections.

2. Summarize the main idea of each section in about a dozen words or less.

3. Explain how your particular passage (use Jonah 1:13–16 for this exercise) relates to the surrounding context.

Assignment 8-3 (Exegetical Paper)

Passage in Ephesians you were assigned: _____

    1. Outline the book of Ephesians.

2. Discuss briefly how your passage relates to the overall outline. That is, what section does your passage fall in and what does your passage seem to be saying in regard to the larger section in which it occurs?

3. Explain how the paragraph before and the paragraph after your passage relate to the thought of your passage.

NAME _____ DATE _____

The NIV Exhaustive Concordance (also titled *The Strongest NIV Exhaustive Concordance*) that is available at the time of publication of this third edition of *Grasping God's Word* is based on the NIV that came out in 1984. Subsequently a new edition of the NIV has been published (2011), with a significant number of changes in wording. If you are using an NIV 2011, you must be aware that there may be some variances of wording between the concordance and your Bible as you are working on word studies. When the new NIV exhaustive concordance is published based on the NIV 2011, those variances will disappear.

Assignment 9-1

Concordance Exercises

1. Use the concordance to answer the following questions about Acts 1:8.

   a. Write out the English transliterated form of the word translated "power" in Acts 1:8: _____

   b. How many times does this word occur in the New Testament? _____

   c. List the passages in Acts that translate this word as "power":

   d. List the passages in Acts that translate this word as "miracles":

2. Use the concordance to answer the following questions about Exodus 4:21.

   a. Write out the English transliterated form of the word translated "power" in Exodus 4:21: _____

   b. How many times does this word occur in the Old Testament? _____

   c. List the passages in Exodus that translate the word as "power":

3. The NIV uses the word "judge" in 1 Corinthians 4:3, 5; 6:5. Are these the same Greek words?_____

Write out the English transliteration of the three Greek words translated as "judge" in these three passages.

4. Use the concordance to answer the following questions about the word "hope":

a. Paul uses the word "hope" in Romans 4:18. How many times total does Paul use this same word in his letters? _____ (Do *not* assume Paul wrote Hebrews.)

b. How many times is the word used in Matthew, Mark, and Luke?_____

c. Is this the same word for "hope" that is used in 1 Corinthians 13:13? _____

Assignment 9-2

You are studying the Sermon on the Mount (Matthew 5–7) and the word "worry" in Matthew 6 catches your eye. You decide to study the word "worry" more in depth.

1. Use your concordance to find the Greek word that is translated "worry" in Matthew 6:25. Do this by looking up "worry" in the first part of the concordance. Then find "Mt 6:25" in the left column and look to the right to find the G/K number. What is the G/K number of the word translated "worry" in Matthew 6:25? _____

2. Now turn to that number in the "Greek to English Dictionary and Index" in the back of the concordance. Remember, we use the "Hebrew to English Dictionary and Index" for Old Testament words and the "Greek to English Dictionary and Index" for New Testament words. What is the Greek word that is beside that number? Write out the word in transliterated English form _____ (Don't *worry* ☺ about spelling.) How many times is it used in the New Testament? _____

3. While you're looking at the Greek word in the "Greek to English Dictionary and Index," make a list of the different ways the NIV translates this particular Greek word:

   • _____ (5 times)

   • _____ (4 times)

   • _____ (4 times)

   • _____ (2 times)

   • _____ (1 time)

   • _____ (1 time)

   • _____ (1 time)

   • _____ (1 time)

4. Next, look up each translation you listed above in the first part of your concordance and find the chapter and verse where the Greek word is used. For example, the NIV translates the Greek word as "worry about" five times. As you look up "worry about" in the first part of your concordance, you need to make sure that both words ("worry" and "about") are in bold print *and* that the number to the right is the same one that you have already identified. You will discover that the Greek word is translated "worry about" by the NIV in Matthew 6:25, 34; 10:19; Luke 12:11, 22 (5 times). The "worry about" in Luke 12:29 is a different G/K number. Now finish completing the chart below by looking up each translation:

   • "worry about" (5 times)–Matthew 6:25, 34; 10:19; Luke 12:11, 22

   • _____ (4 times)–

   • _____ (4 times)–

   • _____ (2 times)–

   • _____ (1 time)–

   • _____ (1 time)–

   • _____ (1 time)–

   • _____ (1 time)–

5. Now that you know how the NIV translates the word and where it is found in the New Testament, examine each occurrence in context as a means of identifying the word's range of meaning. All this is part of determining what the word *could* mean before you decide what it *does* mean in Matthew 6:25. This step is probably the most important, but also the most difficult. There is an art to identifying a word's semantic range. Don't give up. Keep working at it and you'll find that it gets easier with practice. Answer the following questions about how the word is used in each context as a way of getting at its range of meaning:

a. What things are we told not to worry about in Matthew 6:25, 27, 28, 31, 34; Luke 12:22, 25, 26?

b. What is the context in Matthew 10:19 and Luke 12:11? Is this a different kind of worry than that prohibited in Matthew 6:25?

c. What stands in contrast to Martha's worry (Luke 10:41)? How does this contrast help to define Martha's worry?

d. In 1 Corinthians 7 Paul uses the word four times. Describe the context of this usage.

e. What do the contexts of 1 Corinthians 12 and Philippians 2 have in common?

f. What kind of worry is Paul describing in Philippians 4? How do you know?

6. Based on your brief study of the word as used in context, describe as best you can the semantic range of the word. There are at least two major senses of the word and perhaps a couple of more.

7. Now decide what the Greek word used in Matthew 6:25 and translated "worry" actually means in this verse. Select one of the semantic-range options that you identified in step 6 and explain why you think the word carries that meaning in Matthew 6:25.

8. To check your work, see Verbrugge, *New International Dictionary of New Testament Theology: Abridged Edition*, 364.

Assignment 9-3

You want to study the word "meditate" in Joshua 1:8, where Joshua is told by God: "Keep this Book of the Law always on your lips; meditate on it day and night, so that you may be careful to do everything written in it."

1. Use your concordance to find the Hebrew word that is translated "meditate" in Joshua 1:8. What is the G/K number of that word? _____

2. Now turn to that number in the "Hebrew to English Dictionary and Index" in the back of your concordance. What is the Hebrew word that is beside that number? Write out the word in transliterated English form. _____ How many times is it used in the Old Testament? _____

3. Make a list of the different ways the NIV translates this Hebrew word.

4. Next, look up each translation you listed above in the first part of your concordance and find the chapter and verse where the Hebrew word is used. List those verses beside each usage.

5. Now that you know how the NIV translates the word and where it is found in the Old Testament, examine each occurrence in context as a means of identifying the word's range of meaning.

6. Based on your brief study of the word as used in context, describe as best you can the semantic range of the word.

7. Now decide what the Hebrew word used in Joshua 1:8 means. Select one of the semantic-range options that you identified in step 6 and explain why you think the word carries that meaning in Joshua 1:8.

8. To check your work, see VanGemeren, *New International Dictionary of Old Testament Theology and Exegesis*, 1:1006–8.

Assignment 9-4

Complete the following word study. Follow the example in your textbook for the word "offer" (pp. 180–83).

Word: "trials"	Text: James 1:2–3
Transliteration:	G/K Number:

1. Why study this word?

2. What *could* this word mean (semantic range)? Follow the example on pages 181–82 of your textbook.

3. What *does* this word mean in context? Be sure to discuss your choice. See the discussion on pages 182–83 in your textbook as an example.

Assignment 9-5

Complete the following word study. Follow the example in your textbook for the word "offer" (pp. 181–83) .

Word: "sick"	Text: James 5:14
Transliteration:	G/K Number:

1. Why study this word?

2. What *could* this word mean (semantic range)? Follow the example on pages 181–82 of your textbook.

3. What *does* this word mean in context? Be sure to discuss your choice. See the discussion on pages 182–83 in your textbook as an example.

Assignment 9-6 (Exegetical Paper)

Choose a significant word from the passage in Ephesians that you were assigned and complete a word study on that word. Follow the example in your textbook for the word "offer" (pp. 180–83).

Word:	Text:
Transliteration:	G/K Number:

1. Why study this word?

2. What *could* this word mean (semantic range)? Follow the example on pages 181–82 of your textbook.

3. What *does* this word mean in context? Be sure to discuss your choice. See the discussion on pages 182–83 in your textbook as an example.

PART 3

Meaning and Application

WHO CONTROLS THE MEANING? Chapter 10

NAME _____   DATE _____

Assignment 10-1

Explain the difference between *reader response* and *authorial intent*.

Assignment 10-2

Why is the issue of *communication* important to the discussion of authorial intent?

Assignment 10-3

Discuss several situations whereby a reader may intentionally change an author's intended meaning.

LEVELS OF MEANING Chapter 11

NAME _____ DATE _____

Assignment 11-1

Read 1 Kings 17:1–6 below and use your imagination to develop a far-fetched allegorical interpretation. Ignore the context completely and try to come up with a "superspiritual" meaning for as many of the details as possible. Keep in mind that the point of this exercise is to misinterpret the passage intentionally. Don't be concerned with the real meaning of the passage. Be as creative (and wrong) as you can.

[1]Now Elijah the Tishbite, from Tishbe in Gilead, said to Ahab, "As the LORD, the God of Israel, lives, whom I serve, there will be neither dew nor rain in the next few years except at my word."

[2]Then the word of the LORD came to Elijah: [3]"Leave here, turn eastward and hide in the Kerith Ravine, east of the Jordan. [4]You will drink from the brook, and I have directed the ravens to supply you with food there."

[5]So he did what the LORD had told him. He went to the Kerith Ravine, east of the Jordan, and stayed there. [6]The ravens brought him bread and meat in the morning and bread and meat in the evening, and he drank from the brook.

Far-fetched allegorical interpretation:

Assignment 11-2

Using the ELS Bible Code method described in chapter 11 of the textbook, search the first page of chapter 11 in *Grasping God's Word* to find at least four of the encoded words below. Fill in the blanks as shown in the example.

Procedure summary. Go to the first page of chapter 11 in the textbook. Skip the title "Levels of Meaning" and skip the headings. Start with the bold caption "Introduction" followed by the first word, "does," of the first sentence. Ignore all spaces and verse numbers, but include the Bible text and the reference to "Luke." Continue until the end of the fifth paragraph, the one that ends with "That's why she needed the lamp." You will look at every other letter, then every third letter, every fourth letter, and so forth until you locate the code words below with equal spacing between letters. For each code word identify which regular word it starts in and what the letter spacing is. *On the back side of this assignment sheet, we have presented this text with all of the spaces and punctuation deleted. Use that as a worksheet.*

Example:

Find the ELS encoded word *hot*.

Look in the next to the last paragraph on the first page of this chapter. Observe the sentence that says, "There are more cookies in the kitchen if you need them." Notice the phrase *kitchen if you need them*. Starting with the *h* in *kitchen*, we skip five letters and come to *o* in *you*. Then we skip another five letters and end on *t* in *them*. For our answer we fill in the blanks, writing:

hot, starts with *h* in **kitchen**. Letter spacing of **5**.

Find at least four of the following encoded words and fill in the blanks:

1. *how*, starts with *h* in _____.   Letter spacing of _____.

2. *cow*, starts with *c* in _____.   Letter spacing of _____.

3. *fed*, starts with *f* in _____.   Letter spacing of _____.

4. *lot*, starts with *l* in _____.   Letter spacing of _____.

5. *boom*, starts with *b* in _____.   Letter spacing of _____.

Extra Credit. Find the following encoded word.

6. *mom*, starts with *m* in _____.   Letter spacing of _____.

Identify (dream up) some type of concept connection between *mom* and the sentences that are intersected by this word. As the ELS proponents do, try to develop an argument demonstrating that *mom* did not simply occur here by chance but is prophetically connected to the sentences in which it occurs. Of course, keep in mind that it did occur by chance.

IntroductionDoestheBiblehavedifferent*levels*ofmeaningThatisafterwe
haveseenthesocalledsurfacemeaningorliteralmeaningaretherеanyother
deeperlevelsofspiritualmeaningThischapterwillexplorethisquestionTh
isisnotanesotericissueofconcernonlytoscholarsEveryChristianwhoread
stheBibleandseekstofindGodswillforhisorherlifewillencounterthisissu
eForexampleimagineyourselfataBiblestudywithadozenothercollegestu
dentsItisyourfirsttimetothisstudyandyouareabituncomfortableYouhav
edevouredseveralchocolatechipcookiesandnowyouareconcentratingon
yourMountainDewAtallskinnyguysittingtoyourrightopenswithprayer
YoureprettysurehisnameisJoshbutyouveonlymethimonceAfterprayerh
ereadsthepassagetobediscussedthateveningOrsupposeawomanhastensi
lvercoinsandlosesoneDoesshenotlightalampsweepthehouseandsearchc
arefullyuntilshefindsitAndwhenshefindsitshecallsherfriendsandneighb
orstogetherandsaysRejoicewithmeIhavefoundmylostcoinInthesamewa
yItellyouthereisrejoicinginthepresenceoftheangelsofGodoveronesinne
rwhorepentsLukeOKcontinuesJoshTheresmorecookiesinthekitchenify
ouneedthemandIthinkwehaveanotherbagofDoritosaroundheresomewhe
reSowhatdoyouthinkthispassagemeansWhatisGodtryingtoteachushere
IdontknowbeginsagirlwithblondhairwearingaChrisTomlinTshirtBut
mystudyBiblesaysthatthehousesinthosedayshadlowroofsandfewwindo
wssoitwaskindofhardtoseeinthereThatswhysheneededthelamp

THE ROLE OF THE HOLY SPIRIT Chapter 12

NAME   DATE

Assignment 12-1

Once upon a time there was a man with two PhDs in New Testament studies, both from prestigious universities. His academic credentials were impeccable, and he constantly devoted himself to the study of the New Testament. The Gospels were his specialty. He did not, however, claim to follow Jesus Christ as Lord and Savior. The professor's wife was a mature believer, with "only" an MA in biblical studies. They had a nine-year-old daughter who had just returned from a Christian children's camp, where she made the decision to give her life to Christ.

In light of what you have learned in this chapter about the Spirit's role in biblical interpretation, describe how each member of the family might approach John 3:16: "For God so loved the world that he gave his one and only Son, that whoever believes in him shall not perish but have eternal life." Write at least one paragraph from the perspective of each family member.

Assignment 12-2

Select one of the following passages and walk through the *lectio divina* exercise described in this chapter. Write a one- to two-page reflection of what this experience meant to you.

Worship: Psalm 100

Worry: Matthew 6:31–33 or 1 Peter 5:6–7

Temptation: 1 Corinthians 10:12–13

Sin and confession: Psalm 51:1–10

Freedom from condemnation: Romans 8:1–4

Abiding: John 15:1–5

Rest: Psalm 62:5–8

Renewing of the mind: Romans 12:1–2

APPLICATION   Chapter 13

NAME   DATE

Assignment 13-1

In chapter 13 of the textbook, we have written two real-world scenarios paralleling the biblical situation of Philippians 4:13 (the student and the single mother). Create another real-world scenario that parallels Philippians 4:13. Remember, when we say *parallel situation*, we mean a situation that contains *all* of the key elements that you identified in Step 5 of chapter 13.

Assignment 13-2

Read Jesus' parable of the good Samaritan in Luke 10:30–35. Contemporize the parable by writing a story of your own that retells the original story so that the effect on the contemporary audience is equivalent to the effect on the original audience. Use the back of this page if necessary.

Assignment 13-3

First Timothy 6:10a reads, "For the love of money is a root of all kinds of evil." Take this verse through the Interpretive Journey, including the application process:

1. Grasp the text in their town. Summarize the original situation and the meaning of the text for the biblical audience.

2. Measure the width of the river. What are the differences between the biblical situation and our situation?

3. Cross the principlizing bridge. List the theological principles communicated by the passage.

4. Consult the biblical map. How does our theological principle fit with the rest of the Bible?

5. Grasp the text in our town. How should Christians today live out the theological principles?

   a. Observe how the principles in the text address the original situation.

   b. Discover a parallel situation in a contemporary context.

   c. Make your applications specific by creating real-world scenarios or by contemporizing.

PART 4

The Interpretive Journey — New Testament

NEW TESTAMENT—LETTERS Chapter 14

NAME _____   DATE _____

Assignment 14-1

When it comes to letters, we need to be able to trace the author's flow of thought. The first step is to see how paragraphs relate to surrounding paragraphs. Write out your answer to the following questions as a way of gaining experience at tracing the author's flow of thought:

1. How does Philippians 2:1–4 relate to Philippians 2:5–11?

2. What is the connection between Ephesians 5:15–21 and Ephesians 5:22–6:9?

3. What role does 1 Corinthians 13 play in the larger unit of 1 Corinthians 12–14?

Assignment 14-2

Choose and check one of the passages below

- ☐ Romans 8:26–27
- ☐ 1 Corinthians 11:27–32
- ☐ Galatians 5:16–18
- ☐ Colossians 3:1–4
- ☐ 2 Timothy 3:16–17
- ☐ Hebrews 4:12–13
- ☐ 1 Peter 5:6–7

Now take the passage you have chosen through all five steps of the Interpretive Journey as explained and illustrated in chapter 14. Do this by answering the following five questions:

Step 1: Grasp the text in their town. What did the text mean to the biblical audience?

Step 2: Measure the width of the river to cross. What are the differences between the biblical audience and us?

Step 3: Cross the principlizing bridge. What is the theological principle in this text?

Step 4: Consult the biblical map. How does our theological principle fit with the rest of the Bible?

Step 5: Grasp the text in our town. How should individual Christians today live out the theological principle?

NAME _____   DATE _____

Assignment 15-1

Apply the two interpretive questions we used to read the gospels to Matthew 24:43–25:13 or to another section of the Gospels selected by your teacher. Record your findings in the chart below.

Matthew 24:43–44	Matthew 24:45–51	Matthew 25:1–13

Assignment 15-2

Interpret the parable of the great banquet in Luke 14:15–24 or the parable of the unjust judge and the persistent widow in Luke 18:1–8 according to the interpretive principles explained in chapter 15 in the section dealing with parables.

Assignment 15-3

Jesus' favorite teaching topic was the kingdom of God. By reading one or both of the following articles on the kingdom of God in the teachings of Jesus, your understanding of the Gospels will be greatly enhanced:

Fee, Gordon D., and Douglas Stuart. "A Final, Very Important Word," in *How to Read the Bible for All Its Worth*, 3rd ed. (Grand Rapids: Zondervan, 2003), 145–48.

Stein, Robert H. "The Content of Jesus' Teaching: The Kingdom of God," in *The Method and Message of Jesus' Teaching*, rev. ed. (Louisville: Westminster John Knox, 1994), 60–81.

NEW TESTAMENT—ACTS Chapter 16

NAME   DATE

Assignment 16-1

Choose and check one of the passages below:

- ☐ Acts 2:42–47
- ☐ Acts 6:1–7
- ☐ Acts 13:1–3
- ☐ Acts 15:1–21
- ☐ Acts 17:16–34

Now take the passage you have chosen through all five steps of the Interpretive Journey as explained and illustrated in chapter 14. Do this by answering the following five questions:

Step 1: Grasp the text in their town. What did the text mean to the biblical audience?

Step 2: Measure the width of the river to cross. What are the differences between the biblical audience and us?

Step 3: Cross the principlizing bridge. What is the theological principle in this text?

Step 4: Consult the biblical map. How does our theological principle fit with the rest of the Bible?

Step 5: Grasp the text in our town. How should individual Christians today live out the theological principle?

NEW TESTAMENT — REVELATION   Chapter 17

NAME ▮▮▮▮▮▮▮▮▮▮▮▮▮▮▮▮▮▮▮▮▮▮   DATE ▮▮▮▮▮▮▮▮▮▮▮▮▮▮

Assignment 17-1

Read the entire book of Revelation and write a one-line description of the main idea of each chapter of the book. For example, for Revelation 1 you might write, "John's vision of the glorified Christ among the churches."

Revelation 1 _____

Revelation 2 _____

Revelation 3 _____

Revelation 4 _____

Revelation 5 _____

Revelation 6 _____

Revelation 7 _____

Revelation 8 _____

Revelation 9 _____

Revelation 10 _____

Revelation 11 _____

Revelation 12 _____

Revelation 13 _____

Revelation 14 _____

Revelation 15 _____

Revelation 16 _____

Revelation 17 _____

Revelation 18 _____

Revelation 19 _____

Revelation 20 _____

Revelation 21 _____

Revelation 22 _____

Assignment 17-2

In Revelation 2–3 we find messages from Jesus Christ to seven churches in Asia Minor. Fill in the chart below showing the message to each of these churches in terms of the (1) command to write, (2) description of Jesus, (3) commendation or praise, (4) complaint or rebuke, (5) exhortation or warning, and (6) promise. Then add an eighth church to the chart—your home church. Write out the message you think Christ would speak to your church for each of the six areas.

Church	Ephesus (2:1–7)	Smyrna (2:8–11)	Pergamum (2:12–17)	Thyatira (2:18–29)
Command				
Jesus				
Praise				
Complaint				
Warning				
Promise				

Church	Sardis (3:1–6)	Philadelphia (3:7–13)	Laodicea (3:14–22)	My Church
Command				
Jesus				
Praise				
Complaint				
Warning				
Promise				

Assignment 17-3

Read again the section in chapter 17 on Revelation 12:1–17 and the Interpretive Journey. In Step 3 (crossing the principlizing bridge) we listed four theological principles or truths that emerge from Revelation 12:1–17. We used the third principle to illustrate the application process. Create a real-world scenario for the first, second, or fourth principle to make a specific application. Write out your real-world scenario.

PART 5

The Interpretive Journey — Old Testament

OLD TESTAMENT—NARRATIVE   Chapter 18

NAME   DATE

Assignment 18-1

First, study 1 Samuel 3:1–21, printed below, and make as many observations as you can. Mark the observations on the text and in the margins. Use additional paper as needed. Then identify the literary context and the historical context. That is, explain how this narrative fits into the overall story of the book. Use a Bible dictionary or commentary if necessary to help you determine the main story line of the book. Next take the Interpretive Journey. Complete each of the five steps below, writing out one or more statements for each step.

[1]The boy Samuel ministered before the Lord under Eli. In those days the word of the Lord was rare; there were not many visions.

[2]One night Eli, whose eyes were becoming so weak that he could barely see, was lying down in his usual place. [3]The lamp of God had not yet gone out, and Samuel was lying down in the house of the Lord, where the ark of God was. [4]Then the Lord called Samuel.

Samuel answered, "Here I am." [5]And he ran to Eli and said, "Here I am; you called me."

But Eli said, "I did not call; go back and lie down." So he went and lay down.

[6]Again the Lord called, "Samuel!" And Samuel got up and went to Eli and said, "Here I am; you called me."

"My son," Eli said, "I did not call; go back and lie down."

[7]Now Samuel did not yet know the Lord: The word of the Lord had not yet been revealed to him.

[8]A third time the Lord called, "Samuel!" And Samuel got up and went to Eli and said, "Here I am; you called me."

Then Eli realized that the Lord was calling the boy. [9]So Eli told Samuel, "Go and lie down, and if he calls you, say, 'Speak, Lord, for your servant is listening.'" So Samuel went and lay down in his place.

[10]The Lord came and stood there, calling as at the other times, "Samuel! Samuel!"

Then Samuel said, "Speak, for your servant is listening."

[11]And the Lord said to Samuel: "See, I am about to do something in Israel that will make the ears of

everyone who hears about it tingle. [12]At that time I will carry out against Eli everything I spoke against his family—from beginning to end. [13]For I told him that I would judge his family forever because of the sin he knew about; his sons blasphemed God, and he failed to restrain them. [14]Therefore, I swore to the house of Eli, 'The guilt of Eli's house will never be atoned for by sacrifice or offering.'"

[15]Samuel lay down until morning and then opened the doors of the house of the LORD. He was afraid to tell Eli the vision, [16]but Eli called him and said, "Samuel, my son."

Samuel answered, "Here I am."

[17]"What was it he said to you?" Eli asked. "Do not hide it from me. May God deal with you, be it ever so severely, if you hide from me anything he told you." [18]So Samuel told him everything, hiding nothing from him. Then Eli said, "He is the LORD; let him do what is good in his eyes."

[19]The LORD was with Samuel as he grew up, and he let none of Samuel's words fall to the ground. [20]And all Israel from Dan to Beersheba recognized that Samuel was attested as a prophet of the LORD. [21]The LORD continued to appear at Shiloh, and there he revealed himself to Samuel through his word.

1. Literary Context:

2. Historical Context:

3. Interpretive Journey:

   Step 1: Grasp the text in their town. What did the text mean to the biblical audience?

   Step 2: Measure the width of the river to cross. What are the differences between the biblical audience and us?

   Step 3: Cross the principlizing bridge. What is the theological principle in this text?

Step 4: Consult the biblical map. How does our theological principle fit with the rest of the Bible? Does the New Testament modify or qualify this principle, and if so, how?

Step 5: Grasp the text in our town. How should individual Christians today live out this modified theological principle?

Assignment 18-2

First, study Genesis 22:1–19, printed below, and make as many observations as you can. Mark the observations on the text and in the margins. Use additional paper as needed. Then identify the literary context and the historical context. That is, explain how this narrative fits into the overall story of the book. Use a Bible dictionary or commentary if necessary to help you determine the main story line of the book. Next take the Interpretive Journey. Complete each of the five steps below, writing out one or more statements for each step.

[1]Some time later God tested Abraham. He said to him, "Abraham!"

"Here I am," he replied.

[2]Then God said, "Take your son, your only son, whom you love—Isaac—and go to the region of Moriah. Sacrifice him there as a burnt offering on a mountain I will show you."

[3]Early the next morning Abraham got up and loaded his donkey. He took with him two of his servants and his son Isaac. When he had cut enough wood for the burnt offering, he set out for the place God had told him about. [4]On the third day Abraham looked up and saw the place in the distance. [5]He said to his servants, "Stay here with the donkey while I and the boy go over there. We will worship and then we will come back to you."

[6]Abraham took the wood for the burnt offering and placed it on his son Isaac, and he himself carried the fire and the knife. As the two of them went on together, [7]Isaac spoke up and said to his father Abraham, "Father?"

"Yes, my son?" Abraham replied.

"The fire and wood are here," Isaac said, "but where is the lamb for the burnt offering?"

[8]Abraham answered, "God himself will provide the lamb for the burnt offering, my son." And the two of them went on together.

[9]When they reached the place God had told him about, Abraham built an altar there and arranged the wood on it. He bound his son Isaac and laid him on the altar, on top of the wood. [10]Then he reached out his hand and took the knife to slay his son. [11]But the angel of the LORD called out to him from heaven, "Abraham! Abraham!"

"Here I am," he replied.

[12]"Do not lay a hand on the boy," he said. "Do not do anything to him. Now I know that you fear God, because you have not withheld from me your son, your only son."

[13]Abraham looked up and there in a thicket he saw a ram caught by its horns. He went over and took the ram

and sacrificed it as a burnt offering instead of his son. ¹⁴So Abraham called that place The Lᴏʀᴅ Will Provide. And to this day it is said, "On the mountain of the Lᴏʀᴅ it will be provided."

¹⁵The angel of the Lᴏʀᴅ called to Abraham from heaven a second time ¹⁶and said, "I swear by myself, declares the Lᴏʀᴅ, that because you have done this and have not withheld your son, your only son, ¹⁷I will surely bless you and make your descendants as numerous as the stars in the sky and as the sand on the seashore. Your descendants will take possession of the cities of their enemies, ¹⁸and through your offspring all nations on earth will be blessed, because you have obeyed me."

¹⁹Then Abraham returned to his servants, and they set off together for Beersheba. And Abraham stayed in Beersheba.

1. Literary Context:

2. Historical Context:

3. Interpretive Journey:

   Step 1: Grasp the text in their town. What did the text mean to the biblical audience?

Step 2: Measure the width of the river to cross. What are the differences between the biblical audience and us?

Step 3: Cross the principlizing bridge. What is the theological principle in this text?

Step 4: Consult the biblical map. How does our theological principle fit with the rest of the Bible? Does the New Testament modify or qualify this principle, and if so, how?

Step 5: Grasp the text in our town. How should individual Christians today live out this modified theological principle?

Assignment 18-3

As background, read Deuteronomy 17:14–17 (rules for the king) and 1 Samuel 8:10–18 (warnings about the king). Now read the story of Solomon (1 Kings 1–11). Discuss the ways in which Solomon violates the rules for the king and how he fulfills the warnings. Contrast his good deeds with his bad deeds. In the narrator's mind, is Solomon a good character or a bad character? Is he a hero or a bum?

OLD TESTAMENT—LAW Chapter 19

NAME   DATE

Assignment 19-1

Study Leviticus 26:1, printed below, and make as many observations as you can. Mark the observations on the text and in the margins. Be sure you understand the meanings of all of the words. Do background study and word studies as needed to understand each term. Next, identify the historical-cultural context and the literary context. When and where is this law given? What does the surrounding text discuss? Finally, take the Interpretive Journey, completing each of the five steps below. Write out one or more statements for each step.

> Do not make idols or set up an image or a sacred stone for yourselves, and do not place a carved stone in your land to bow down before it. I am the LORD your God.

1. Historical-Cultural Context:

2. Literary Context:

3. Interpretive Journey:

   Step 1: Grasp the text in their town. What did the text mean to the biblical audience?

Step 2: Measure the width of the river to cross. What are the differences between the biblical audience and us?

Step 3: Cross the principlizing bridge. What is the theological principle in this text?

Step 4: Consult the biblical map. How does our theological principle fit with the rest of the Bible? Does the New Testament modify or qualify this principle, and if so, how?

Step 5: Grasp the text in our town. How should individual Christians today live out this modified theological principle?

Assignment 19-2

Study Leviticus 23:22, printed below, and make as many observations as you can. Mark the observations on the text and in the margins. Be sure that you understand the meanings of all of the words. Do background study and word studies as needed to understand each term. Next, identify the historical-cultural context and the literary context. When and where is this law given? What does the surrounding text discuss? Finally, take the Interpretive Journey, completing each of the five steps below. Write out one or more statements for each step.

When you reap the harvest of your land, do not reap to the very edges of your field or gather the

gleanings of your harvest. Leave them for the poor and for the foreigner residing among you. I am the

LORD your God.

1. Historical-Cultural Context:

2. Literary Context:

3. Interpretive Journey:

   Step 1: Grasp the text in their town. What did the text mean to the biblical audience?

Step 2: Measure the width of the river to cross. What are the differences between the biblical audience and us?

Step 3: Cross the principlizing bridge. What is the theological principle in this text?

Step 4: Consult the biblical map. How does our theological principle fit with the rest of the Bible? Does the New Testament modify or qualify this principle, and if so, how?

Step 5: Grasp the text in our town. How should individual Christians today live out this modified theological principle?

Assignment 19-3

Study Numbers 15:17–21, printed below, and make as many observations as you can. Mark the observations on the text and in the margins. Be sure that you understand the meanings of all of the words. Do background study and word studies as needed to understand each term. Next, identify the historical-cultural context and the literary context. When and where is this law given? What does the surrounding text discuss? Finally, take the Interpretive Journey, completing each of the five steps below. Write out one or more statements for each step.

The LORD said to Moses, "Speak to the Israelites and say to them: 'When you enter the land to

which I am taking you and you eat the food of the land, present a portion as an offering to the LORD.

Present a loaf from the first of your ground meal and present it as an offering from the threshing floor.

Throughout the generations to come you are to give this offering to the LORD from the first of your

ground meal."

1. Historical-Cultural Context:

2. Literary Context:

3. Interpretive Journey:

   Step 1: Grasp the text in their town. What did the text mean to the biblical audience?

Step 2: Measure the width of the river to cross. What are the differences between the biblical audience and us?

Step 3: Cross the principlizing bridge. What is the theological principle in this text?

Step 4: Consult the biblical map. How does our theological principle fit with the rest of the Bible? Does the New Testament modify or qualify this principle, and if so, how?

Step 5: Grasp the text in our town. How should individual Christians today live out this modified theological principle?

Assignment 19-4

Study Deuteronomy 22:8, printed below, and make as many observations as you can. Mark the observations on the text and in the margins. Be sure that you understand the meanings of all of the words. Do background study and word studies as needed to understand each term. Next, identify the historical-cultural context and the literary context. When and where is this law given? What does the surrounding text discuss? Finally, take the Interpretive Journey, completing each of the five steps below. Write out one or more statements for each step.

> When you build a new house, make a parapet around your roof so that you may not bring the guilt of
>
> bloodshed on your house if someone falls from the roof.

1. Historical-Cultural Context:

2. Literary Context:

3. Interpretive Journey:

   Step 1: Grasp the text in their town. What did the text mean to the biblical audience?

Step 2: Measure the width of the river to cross. What are the differences between the biblical audience and us?

Step 3: Cross the principlizing bridge. What is the theological principle in this text?

Step 4: Consult the biblical map. How does our theological principle fit with the rest of the Bible? Does the New Testament modify or qualify this principle, and if so, how?

Step 5: Grasp the text in our town. How should individual Christians today live out this modified theological principle?

Assignment 19-5

Study Leviticus 23:3, printed below, and make as many observations as you can. Mark the observations on the text and in the margins. Be sure that you understand the meanings of all of the words. Do background study and word studies as needed to understand each term. Next, identify the historical-cultural context and the literary context. When and where is this law given? What does the surrounding text discuss? Finally, take the Interpretive Journey, completing each of the five steps below. Write out one or more statements for each step.

There are six days when you may work, but the seventh day is a day of sabbath rest, a day of sacred

assembly. You are not to do any work; wherever you live, it is a sabbath to the LORD.

1. Historical-Cultural Context:

2. Literary Context:

3. Interpretive Journey:

   Step 1: Grasp the text in their town. What did the text mean to the biblical audience?

Step 2: Measure the width of the river to cross. What are the differences between the biblical audience and us?

Step 3: Cross the principlizing bridge. What is the theological principle in this text?

Step 4: Consult the biblical map. How does our theological principle fit with the rest of the Bible? Does the New Testament modify or qualify this principle, and if so, how?

Step 5: Grasp the text in our town. How should individual Christians today live out this modified theological principle?

OLD TESTAMENT—POETRY   Chapter 20

NAME   DATE

Assignment 20-1

Based on the discussion of parallelism in the textbook, classify each of the couplets (verses) in Psalm 20, printed below. That is, identify each set of parallel lines as *synonymous*, *developmental*, *illustrative*, *contrastive*, or *formal*. Note that verses 5 and 6 each have three lines instead of two. Either classify all three lines together as one category, or classify the first two as one category and then relate the last line to the first two as a category. Verse 1 has been completed as an example for you.

¹May the LORD answer you when you are in distress;

    may the name of the God of Jacob protect you.   *Developmental*

²May he send you help from the sanctuary

    and grant you support from Zion.   _____

³May he remember all your sacrifices

    and accept your burnt offerings.   _____

⁴May he give you the desire of your heart

    and make all your plans succeed.   _____

⁵May we shout for joy over your victory

    and lift up our banners in the name of our God.   _____

May the LORD grant all your requests.   _____

⁶Now this I know: the LORD gives victory to his anointed.

    He answers him from his heavenly sanctuary   _____

    with the victorious power of his right hand.   _____

[7]Some trust in chariots and some in horses,

but we trust in the name of the Lord our God.   _____

[8]They are brought to their knees and fall,

but we rise up and stand firm.   _____

[9] Lord, give victory to the king!

Answer us when we call!   _____

Assignment 20-2

For each of the figures of speech in Psalm 102:1–14, listed below, classify the figure according to the categories discussed in the textbook (simile, metaphor, indirect analogy, etc.). Sometimes there are two or three possible answers for the classification; choose the one you think is most accurate. Then explain what the figure or image means. The first one has been done for you.

102:1b	cry	Classification—indirect analogy
		Explanation—The psalmist is comparing his prayer to a cry.
102:2a	face	Classification
		Explanation
102:2b	ear	Classification
		Explanation
102:3a	days/smoke	Classification
		Explanation
102:3b	bones/embers	Classification
		Explanation
102:4a	heart/grass	Classification
		Explanation
102:5b	skin/bones	Classification
		Explanation
102:6	owl	Classification
		Explanation
102:7	bird	Classification
		Explanation
102:9a	ashes/food	Classification
		Explanation
102:9b	drink/tears	Classification
		Explanation
102:11a	days/shadow	Classification
		Explanation
102:11b	grass	Classification
		Explanation
102:13a	arise	Classification
		Explanation
102:14a	stones	Classification
		Explanation
102:14b	dust	Classification
		Explanation

Assignment 20-3

Take the Interpretive Journey with Psalm 1, printed below. Follow the directions, completing all three parts of the assignment.

1. Read through Psalm 1 several times. Find and mark as many observations as you can on the text below.

> [1]Blessed is the one
>
> who does not walk in step with the wicked
>
> or stand in the way that sinners take
>
> or sit in the company of mockers,
>
> [2]but whose delight is in the law of the LORD,
>
> and who meditates on his law day and night.
>
> [3]That person is like a tree planted by streams of water,
>
> which yields its fruit in season
>
> and whose leaf does not wither—
>
> whatever they do prospers.
>
> [4]Not so the wicked!
>
> They are like chaff
>
> that the wind blows away.
>
> [5]Therefore the wicked will not stand in the judgment,
>
> nor sinners in the assembly of the righteous.
>
> [6]For the LORD watches over the way of the righteous,
>
> but the way of the wicked leads to destruction.

2. Describe and define the figures of speech in each verse.

   Verse 1:

   Verse 2:

   Verse 3:

   Verse 4:

   Verse 5:

   Verse 6:

3. Make the Interpretive Journey by completing the following:

Step 1: Grasp the text in their town. What did the text mean to the biblical audience?

Step 2: Measure the width of the river to cross. What are the differences between the biblical audience and us?

Step 3: Cross the principlizing bridge. What is the theological principle in this text?

Step 4: Consult the biblical map. How does our theological principle fit with the rest of the Bible? Does the New Testament modify or qualify this principle, and if so, how?

Step 5: Grasp the text in our town. How should individual Christians today live out this modified theological principle?

OLD TESTAMENTS—PROPHETS   Chapter 21

NAME _____   DATE _____

Assignment 21-1

First, study Micah 6:6–8, printed below, and make as many observations as you can. Mark your observations on the text and in the margins. Be sure that you understand the meanings of all of the words. Do a background study and word studies as needed to understand each term. Be sure to identify all figures of speech. Then answer the specific questions listed under Step 1 and write a paragraph for each of the other steps to complete the Interpretive Journey.

> ⁶With what shall I come before the Lord
>
> and bow down before the exalted God?
>
> Shall I come before him with burnt offerings,
>
> with calves a year old?
>
> ⁷Will the Lord be pleased with thousands of rams,
>
> with ten thousand rivers of olive oil?
>
> Shall I offer my firstborn for my transgression,
>
> the fruit of my body for the sin of my soul?
>
> ⁸He has shown you, O mortal, what is good.
>
> And what does the Lord require of you?
>
> To act justly and to love mercy
>
> and to walk humbly with your God.

Step 1: Grasp the text in their town. What did the text mean to the biblical audience? Identify the historical-cultural context and the literary context of Micah 6:6–8. When and where does this prophecy occur? (Use a Bible dictionary or commentary to help you with this, if necessary.) What does the surrounding text discuss? Does this passage fall into one of the three main points of the prophetic message or one of the indictments discussed in the text? If so, which one? Review the discussion regarding the point of the prophetic message that relates to your passage.

Step 2: Measure the width of the river to cross. What are the differences between the biblical audience and us?

Step 3: Cross the principlizing bridge. What is the theological principle in this text?

Step 4: Consult the biblical map. How does our theological principle fit with the rest of the Bible? Does the New Testament modify or qualify this principle, and if so, how?

Step 5: Grasp the text in our town. How should individual Christians today live out this modified theological principle?

Assignment 21-2

Study Jeremiah 7:1–7, printed below, and make as many observations as you can. Mark your observations on the text and in the margins. Be sure that you understand the meanings of all of the words. Do background study and word studies as needed to understand each term. Be sure to identify all figures of speech. Then answer the specific questions listed under Step 1 and write a paragraph for each of the other steps to complete the Interpretive Journey.

[1]This is the word that came to Jeremiah from the LORD: [2]"Stand at the gate of the LORD's house and there proclaim this message:

"'Hear the word of the LORD, all you people of Judah who come through these gates to worship the LORD. [3]This is what the LORD Almighty, the God of Israel, says: Reform your ways and your actions, and I will let you live in this place. [4]Do not trust in deceptive words and say, "This is the temple of the LORD, the temple of the LORD, the temple of the LORD!" [5]If you really change your ways and your actions and deal with each other justly, [6]if you do not oppress the foreigner, the fatherless or the widow and do not shed innocent blood in this place, and if you do not follow other gods to your own harm, [7]then I will let you live in this place, in the land I gave your ancestors for ever and ever.'"

Step 1: Grasp the text in their town. What did the text mean to the biblical audience? Identify the historical-cultural context and the literary context of Jeremiah 7:1–7. When and where does this prophecy occur? (Use a Bible dictionary or commentary to help you with this, if necessary.) What does the surrounding text discuss? Does this passage fall into one of the three main points of the prophetic message or one of the indictments discussed in the text? If so, which one? Review the discussion regarding the point of the prophetic message that relates to your passage.

Step 2: Measure the width of the river to cross. What are the differences between the biblical audience and us?

Step 3: Cross the principlizing bridge. What is the theological principle in this text?

Step 4: Consult the biblical map. How does our theological principle fit with the rest of the Bible? Does the New Testament modify or qualify this principle, and if so, how?

Step 5: Grasp the text in our town. How should individual Christians today live out this modified theological principle?

Assignment 21-3

Study Jeremiah 31:10–14, printed below, and make as many observations as you can. Mark your observations on the text and in the margins. Be sure that you understand the meanings of all of the words. Do background study and word studies as needed to understand each term. Be sure to identify all figures of speech. Then answer the specific questions listed under Step 1 and write a paragraph for each of the other steps to complete the Interpretive Journey.

> ^{10}"Hear the word of the Lord, you nations;
>
> proclaim it in distant coastlands:
>
> 'He who scattered Israel will gather them
>
> and will watch over his flock like a shepherd.'
>
> ^{11}For the Lord will deliver Jacob
>
> and redeem them from the hand of those stronger than they.
>
> ^{12}They will come and shout for joy on the heights of Zion;
>
> they will rejoice in the bounty of the Lord—
>
> the grain, the new wine and the olive oil,
>
> the young of the flocks and herds.
>
> They will be like a well-watered garden,
>
> and they will sorrow no more.
>
> ^{13}Then young women will dance and be glad,
>
> young men and old as well.
>
> I will turn their mourning into gladness;
>
> I will give them comfort and joy instead of sorrow.
>
> ^{14}I will satisfy the priests with abundance,
>
> and my people will be filled with my bounty,"
>
> declares the Lord.

Step 1: Grasp the text in their town. What did the text mean to the biblical audience? Identify the historical-cultural context and the literary context of Jeremiah 31:10–14. When and where does this prophecy occur? (Use a Bible dictionary or commentary to help you with this, if necessary.) What does the surrounding text discuss? Does this passage fall into one of the three main points of the prophetic message or one of the indictments discussed in the text? If so, which one? Review the discussion regarding the point of the prophetic message that relates to your passage.

Step 2: Measure the width of the river to cross. What are the differences between the biblical audience and us?

Step 3: Cross the principlizing bridge. What is the theological principle in this text?

Step 4: Consult the biblical map. How does our theological principle fit with the rest of the Bible? Does the New Testament modify or qualify this principle, and if so, how?

Step 5: Grasp the text in our town. How should individual Christians today live out this modified theological principle?

OLD TESTAMENT — WISDOM | Chapter 22

NAME _____   DATE _____

Assignment 22-1

Take the Interpretive Journey with each of the proverbs listed below. That is, take the first proverb and then write a short paragraph for each of the five steps regarding that proverb. Then turn to the next proverb and complete the five steps for it, followed by the same procedure for the last proverb. Try to make the application in Step 5 a real application for your life.

Proverbs 10:12

Hatred stirs up conflict,

but love covers over all wrongs.

Step 1: Grasp the text in their town. What did the text mean to the biblical audience?

Step 2: Measure the width of the river to cross. What are the differences between the biblical audience and us?

Step 3: Cross the principlizing bridge. What is the theological principle in this text?

Step 4: Consult the biblical map. How does our theological principle fit with the rest of the Bible? Does the New Testament modify or qualify this principle, and if so, how?

Step 5: Grasp the text in our town. How should individual Christians today live out this modified theological principle?

Proverbs 11:1

> The LORD detests dishonest scales,
>
> but accurate weights find favor with him.

Step 1: Grasp the text in their town. What did the text mean to the biblical audience?

Step 2: Measure the width of the river to cross. What are the differences between the biblical audience and us?

Step 3: Cross the principlizing bridge. What is the theological principle in this text?

Step 4: Consult the biblical map. How does our theological principle fit with the rest of the Bible? Does the New Testament modify or qualify this principle, and if so, how?

Step 5: Grasp the text in our town. How should individual Christians today live out this modified theological principle?

Proverbs 18:24

> One who has unreliable friends soon comes to ruin,
>
> but there is a friend who sticks closer than a brother.

Step 1: Grasp the text in their town. What did the text mean to the biblical audience?

Step 2: Measure the width of the river to cross. What are the differences between the biblical audience and us?

Step 3: Cross the principlizing bridge. What is the theological principle in this text?

Step 4: Consult the biblical map. How does our theological principle fit with the rest of the Bible? Does the New Testament modify or qualify this principle, and if so, how?

Step 5: Grasp the text in our town. How should individual Christians today live out this modified theological principle?

Assignment 22-2

Take the Interpretive Journey with Job 38:18–21, printed below. That is, write a short paragraph for each of the five steps of the Journey. Be sure that you include a discussion of literary context as part of Step 1—that is, identify where in the overall story of Job this passage occurs. Identify who is speaking to whom in this text and what is occurring in the chapters that surround this text. Then complete the rest of the Journey.

> [18]Have you comprehended the vast expanses of the earth?
>
> Tell me, if you know all this.
>
> [19]What is the way to the abode of light?
>
> And where does darkness reside?
>
> [20]Can you take them to their places?
>
> Do you know the paths to their dwellings?
>
> [21]Surely you know, for you were already born!
>
> You have lived so many years!

Step 1: Grasp the text in their town. What did the text mean to the biblical audience?

Step 2: Measure the width of the river to cross. What are the differences between the biblical audience and us?

Step 3: Cross the principlizing bridge. What is the theological principle in this text?

Step 4: Consult the biblical map. How does our theological principle fit with the rest of the Bible? Does the New Testament modify or qualify this principle, and if so, how?

Step 5: Grasp the text in our town. How should individual Christians today live out this modified theological principle?

THE EXEGETICAL PAPER
On a Passage from Ephesians

THE EXEGETICAL PAPER ON A PASSAGE FROM EPHESIANS

NAME _____   DATE _____

These guidelines assume that you are using *Grasping God's Word* to learn how to read, interpret, and apply the Bible. As a result, we will focus below on how to present the results of your interpretive work. Teachers have personal preferences when it comes to writing exegetical papers (e.g., footnotes or endnotes?). Our guidelines present the basics related to form and content that should prove helpful.

Form

The paper is to be typed, using double spacing, a twelve-point font and one-inch margins. The minimum length is nine pages; the maximum is thirteen pages (excluding the title page and the bibliography).

Citations should be referenced in accordance with the guidelines of the style manual that your teacher prefers. Commonly used style manuals for writing exegetical papers include:

Hudson, Bob, gen. ed. *A Christian Writer's Manual of Style*. Updated and exp. ed. Grand Rapids: Zondervan, 2004.

Turabian, Kate. *A Manual for Writers of Term Papers, Theses, and Dissertations*. 7th ed. Chicago: University of Chicago Press, 2007.

Vyhmeister, Nancy J. *Quality Research Papers: For Students of Religion and Theology*. 2nd ed. Grand Rapids: Zondervan, 2008.

Content

1. Title Page (1 page)

The title page should clearly state which passage from Ephesians you are exegeting, the course title, the professor's name, the date submitted, and your name.

2. Main Idea and Outline (1 page)

Identify the text from Ephesians you have been assigned and summarize its main idea in one sentence. Then present a full outline of your passage, showing how the main idea unfolds. For each main point of your outline, show in parentheses that main verses correspond. All of the verses of your passage should be included in the main points of your outline.

3. Introduction

This paragraph should gain the reader's attention and introduce the main idea of your passage.

4. Context (1–2 pages)

This part consists of two sections. First, include a brief discussion of the historical-cultural context of the book. What do your readers need to know about the biblical author, the original audience, and their world in order to grasp the meaning of the passage?

Second, discuss the literary context of your passage. Describe the author's flow of thought in the book and discuss how your passage fits into and contributes to the flow of thought. Pay particular attention to how your passage relates to the passage that precedes it and the one that follows it.

5. Content (5–8 pages)

This represents the body of your paper and the heart of your exegetical work. You should let the main points of your outline function as subheadings. Include under each subheading a detailed explanation of your passage.

Explain what the text says and what it means in context. Be sure to include significant elements that you discovered as you observed the text and studied the passage's historical-cultural context. Also, explain the meaning of critical words and concepts. Synthesize your own observations with those of the commentaries.

Speaking of commentaries, you must consult and cite at least four of the sources listed in the attached bibliography on Ephesians. Allow these commentaries to assist you, but be careful not to let them dictate what you conclude about the passage. Be critical of your sources and do not be afraid to disagree with commentators.

Keep in mind that the goal of this section is to explain the meaning of the text in context. Discuss the details of the text, but be sure to move beyond mere description of details to show how the details come together to convey meaning.

6. Application (1 page)

Discuss several applications of this passage to contemporary audiences. Be as practical and realistic as possible.

7. Bibliography (1 page)

Present a formal bibliography of the sources you cite in your paper in accordance with your teacher's preferred style manual.

Checklist

- ☐ I have double-spaced the paper with a twelve-point font and one-inch margins.
- ☐ The paper has a title page.
- ☐ The paper is between nine and thirteen pages long.
- ☐ I have cited sources in accordance with the preferred style manual.
- ☐ My main idea summarizes the entire passage in one sentence.
- ☐ All verses in the passage are included in my outline.
- ☐ My introduction gains the reader's attention and introduces the main idea.
- ☐ I discuss both the historical-cultural and literary contexts.
- ☐ The main points of my outline serve as subheadings in the body of my paper.
- ☐ I explain the meaning of critical words in my passage.
- ☐ I have consulted and cited at least four reputable sources.
- ☐ I discuss several applications of this passage for a contemporary audience.
- ☐ I include a bibliography of sources cited in the paper.
- ☐ I have proofread the paper.

Grading

Grading will be based on the following:

- Form and style (typing, spelling, grammar, etc.)   _____%
- Research (use of sources)   _____%
- Main idea and outline   _____%
- Context (historical and literary)   _____%
- Content   _____%
- Application   _____%

Selected Bibliography on Ephesians

*Arnold, Clinton E. *Ephesians.* Zondervan Exegetical Commentary on the New Testament. Grand Rapids: Zondervan, 2010.

Bruce, F. F. *The Epistle to the Colossians, to Philemon, and to the Ephesians.* New International Commentary on the New Testament. Grand Rapids: Eerdmans, 1984.

Barth, Markus. *Ephesians.* 2 vol. Anchor Bible Commentary. New York: Doubleday, 1974.

Best, Ernest. *Ephesians.* International Critical Commentary. Edinburgh: T&T Clark, 1998.

Hendriksen, William. *Galatians to Ephesians.* Grand Rapids: Baker, 1968.

Hohner, Harold. "Ephesians." In *The Bible Knowledge Commentary.* Wheaton, IL: Victor, 1985.

———. *Ephesians: An Exegetical Commentary.* Grand Rapids: Baker, 2002.

Klein, William W. "Ephesians." In *Expositor's Bible Commentary*, 12:19–173. Grand Rapids: Zondervan, 2006.

Liefeld, Walter L. *Ephesians.* IVP New Testament Commentary Series. Downers Grove, IL: InterVarsity Press, 1997.

Lincoln, Andrew T. *Ephesians.* Word Biblical Commentary. Dallas: Word, 1990.

Martin, Ralph. *Ephesians, Colossians, and Philemon.* Interpretation. Louisville: John Knox, 1991.

O'Brien, Peter T. *The Letter to the Ephesians.* Pillar New Testament Commentary. Grand Rapids: Eerdmans, 1999.

Patzia, Arthur. *Ephesians, Colossians, Philemon.* New International Biblical Commentary. Peabody, MA: Hendrickson, 1984.

Snodgrass, Klyne. *Ephesians.* NIV Application Commentary. Grand Rapids: Zondervan, 1996.

Stott, John R. W. *The Message of Ephesians.* Bible Speaks Today. Downers Grove, IL: InterVarsity Press, 1979.

Thielman, Frank. *Ephesians.* Baker Exegetical Commentary on the New Testament. Grand Rapids: Baker, 2010.

Exegetical Paper Passage Assignments

- ☐ Ephesians 1:3–6
- ☐ Ephesians 1:7–10
- ☐ Ephesians 1:11–14
- ☐ Ephesians 1:15–23
- ☐ Ephesians 2:1–7
- ☐ Ephesians 2:8–13
- ☐ Ephesians 2:14–22
- ☐ Ephesians 3:1–7
- ☐ Ephesians 3:8–13
- ☐ Ephesians 3:14–21
- ☐ Ephesians 4:1–6

- ☐ Ephesians 4:11–16
- ☐ Ephesians 4:17–24
- ☐ Ephesians 4:25–32
- ☐ Ephesians 5:1–6
- ☐ Ephesians 5:7–14
- ☐ Ephesians 5:15–21
- ☐ Ephesians 5:22–33
- ☐ Ephesians 6:1–9
- ☐ Ephesians 6:10–16
- ☐ Ephesians 6:17–20

Ephesians 1:3 – 6

³Praise be to the God and Father of our Lord Jesus Christ, who has blessed us in the heavenly realms with every spiritual blessing in Christ. ⁴For he chose us in him before the creation of the world to be holy and blameless in his sight. In love ⁵he predestined us for adoption to sonship through Jesus Christ, in accordance with his pleasure and will—⁶to the praise of his glorious grace, which he has freely given us in the One he loves.

Ephesians 1:7 – 10

[7]In him we have redemption through his blood, the forgiveness of sins, in accordance with the riches of God's grace [8]that he lavished on us. With all wisdom and understanding, [9]he made known to us the mystery of his will according to his good pleasure, which he purposed in Christ, [10]to be put into effect when the times reach their fulfillment—to bring unity to all things in heaven and on earth under Christ.

Ephesians 1:11 – 14

[11]In him we were also chosen, having been predestined according to the plan of him who works out everything in conformity with the purpose of his will, [12]in order that we, who were the first to put our hope in Christ, might be for the praise of his glory. [13]And you also were included in Christ when you heard the message of truth, the gospel of your salvation. When you believed, you were marked in him with a seal, the promised Holy Spirit, [14]who is a deposit guaranteeing our inheritance until the redemption of those who are God's possession—to the praise of his glory.

Ephesians 1:15 – 23

[15]For this reason, ever since I heard about your faith in the Lord Jesus and your love for all God's people, [16]I have not stopped giving thanks for you, remembering you in my prayers. [17]I keep asking that the God of our Lord Jesus Christ, the glorious Father, may give you the Spirit of wisdom and revelation, so that you may know him better. [18]I pray that the eyes of your heart may be enlightened in order that you may know the hope to which he has called you, the riches of his glorious inheritance in his holy people, [19]and his incomparably great power for us who believe. That power is the same as the mighty strength [20]he exerted when he raised Christ from the dead and seated him at his right hand in the heavenly realms, [21]far above all rule and authority, power and dominion, and every name that is invoked, not only in the present age but also in the one to come. [22]And God placed all things under his feet and appointed him to be head over everything for the church, [23]which is his body, the fullness of him who fills everything in every way.

Ephesians 2:1 – 7

[1]As for you, you were dead in your transgressions and sins, [2]in which you used to live when you followed the ways of this world and of the ruler of the kingdom of the air, the spirit who is now at work in those who are disobedient. [3]All of us also lived among them at one time, gratifying the cravings of our flesh and following its desires and thoughts. Like the rest, we were by nature deserving of wrath. [4]But because of his great love for us, God, who is rich in mercy, [5]made us alive with Christ even when we were dead in transgressions—it is by grace you have been saved. [6]And God raised us up with Christ and seated us with him in the heavenly realms in Christ Jesus, [7]in order that in the coming ages he might show the incomparable riches of his grace, expressed in his kindness to us in Christ Jesus.

Ephesians 2:8 – 13

[8]For it is by grace you have been saved, through faith—and this is not from yourselves, it is the gift of God—[9]not by works, so that no one can boast. [10]For we are God's handiwork, created in Christ Jesus to do good works, which God prepared in advance for us to do.

[11]Therefore, remember that formerly you who are Gentiles by birth and called "uncircumcised" by those who call themselves "the circumcision" (which is done in the body by human hands)— [12]remember that at that time you were separate from Christ, excluded from citizenship in Israel and foreigners to the covenants of the promise, without hope and without God in the world. [13]But now in Christ Jesus you who once were far away have been brought near by the blood of Christ.

Ephesians 2:14 – 22

[14]For he himself is our peace, who has made the two groups one and has destroyed the barrier, the dividing wall of hostility, [15]by setting aside in his flesh the law with its commands and regulations. His purpose was to create in himself one new humanity out of the two, thus making peace, [16]and in one body to reconcile both of them to God through the cross, by which he put to death their hostility. [17]He came and preached peace to you who were far away and peace to those who were near. [18]For through him we both have access to the Father by one Spirit.

[19]Consequently, you are no longer foreigners and strangers, but fellow citizens with God's people and also members of his household, [20]built on the foundation of the apostles and prophets, with Christ Jesus himself as the chief cornerstone. [21]In him the whole building is joined together and rises to become a holy temple in the Lord. [22]And in him you too are being built together to become a dwelling in which God lives by his Spirit.

Ephesians 3:1 – 7

[1]For this reason I, Paul, the prisoner of Christ Jesus for the sake of you Gentiles—

[2]Surely you have heard about the administration of God's grace that was given to me for you, [3]that is, the mystery made known to me by revelation, as I have already written briefly. [4]In reading this, then, you will be able to understand my insight into the mystery of Christ, [5]which was not made known to people in other generations as it has now been revealed by the Spirit to God's holy apostles and prophets. [6]This mystery is that through the gospel the Gentiles are heirs together with Israel, members together of one body, and sharers together in the promise in Christ Jesus.

[7]I became a servant of this gospel by the gift of God's grace given me through the working of his power.

Ephesians 3:8 – 13

[8]Although I am less than the least of all the Lord's people, this grace was given me: to preach to the Gentiles the boundless riches of Christ, [9]and to make plain to everyone the administration of this mystery, which for ages past was kept hidden in God, who created all things. [10]His intent was that now, through the church, the manifold wisdom of God should be made known to the rulers and authorities in the heavenly realms, [11]according to his eternal purpose that he accomplished in Christ Jesus our Lord. [12]In him and through faith in him we may approach God with freedom and confidence. [13]I ask you, therefore, not to be discouraged because of my sufferings for you, which are your glory.

Ephesians 3:14 – 21

[14]For this reason I kneel before the Father, [15]from whom every family in heaven and on earth derives its name. [16]I pray that out of his glorious riches he may strengthen you with power through his Spirit in your inner being, [17]so that Christ may dwell in your hearts through faith. And I pray that you, being rooted and established in love, [18]may have power, together with all the Lord's holy people, to grasp how wide and long and high and deep is the love of Christ, [19]and to know this love that surpasses knowledge — that you may be filled to the measure of all the fullness of God.

[20]Now to him who is able to do immeasurably more than all we ask or imagine, according to his power that is at work within us, [21]to him be glory in the church and in Christ Jesus throughout all generations, for ever and ever! Amen.

Ephesians 4:1 – 6

[1]As a prisoner for the Lord, then, I urge you to live a life worthy of the calling you have received. [2]Be completely humble and gentle; be patient, bearing with one another in love. [3]Make every effort to keep the unity of the Spirit through the bond of peace. [4]There is one body and one Spirit, just as you were called to one hope when you were called; [5]one Lord, one faith, one baptism; [6]one God and Father of all, who is over all and through all and in all.

Ephesians 4:11 – 16

[11]So Christ himself gave the apostles, the prophets, the evangelists, the pastors and teachers, [12]to equip his people for works of service, so that the body of Christ may be built up [13]until we all reach unity in the faith and in the knowledge of the Son of God and become mature, attaining to the whole measure of the fullness of Christ.

[14]Then we will no longer be infants, tossed back and forth by the waves, and blown here and there by every wind of teaching and by the cunning and craftiness of people in their deceitful scheming. [15]Instead, speaking the truth in love, we will grow to become in every respect the mature body of him who is the head, that is, Christ. [16]From him the whole body, joined and held together by every supporting ligament, grows and builds itself up in love, as each part does its work.

Ephesians 4:17 – 24

¹⁷So I tell you this, and insist on it in the Lord, that you must no longer live as the Gentiles do, in the futility of their thinking. ¹⁸They are darkened in their understanding and separated from the life of God because of the ignorance that is in them due to the hardening of their hearts. ¹⁹Having lost all sensitivity, they have given themselves over to sensuality so as to indulge in every kind of impurity, and they are full of greed.

²⁰That, however, is not the way of life you learned ²¹when you heard about Christ and were taught in him in accordance with the truth that is in Jesus.²²You were taught, with regard to your former way of life, to put off your old self, which is being corrupted by its deceitful desires; ²³to be made new in the attitude of your minds; ²⁴and to put on the new self, created to be like God in true righteousness and holiness.

Ephesians 4:25 – 32

[25]Therefore each of you must put off falsehood and speak truthfully to your neighbor, for we are all members of one body. [26]"In your anger do not sin": Do not let the sun go down while you are still angry, [27]and do not give the devil a foothold. [28]Anyone who has been stealing must steal no longer, but must work, doing something useful with their own hands, that they may have something to share with those in need.

[29]Do not let any unwholesome talk come out of your mouths, but only what is helpful for building others up according to their needs, that it may benefit those who listen. [30]And do not grieve the Holy Spirit of God, with whom you were sealed for the day of redemption. [31]Get rid of all bitterness, rage and anger, brawling and slander, along with every form of malice. [32]Be kind and compassionate to one another, forgiving each other, just as in Christ God forgave you.

Ephesians 5:1 – 6

[1]Follow God's example, therefore, as dearly loved children [2]and walk in the way of love, just as Christ loved us and gave himself up for us as a fragrant offering and sacrifice to God.

[3]But among you there must not be even a hint of sexual immorality, or of any kind of impurity, or of greed, because these are improper for God's holy people. [4]Nor should there be obscenity, foolish talk or coarse joking, which are out of place, but rather thanksgiving. [5]For of this you can be sure: No immoral, impure or greedy person—such a person is an idolater—has any inheritance in the kingdom of Christ and of God. [6]Let no one deceive you with empty words, for because of such things God's wrath comes on those who are disobedient.

Ephesians 5:7 – 14

[7]Therefore do not be partners with them. [8]For you were once darkness, but now you are light in the Lord. Live as children of light [9](for the fruit of the light consists in all goodness, righteousness and truth) [10]and find out what pleases the Lord. [11]Have nothing to do with the fruitless deeds of darkness, but rather expose them. [12]It is shameful even to mention what the disobedient do in secret. [13]But everything exposed by the light becomes visible—and everything that is illuminated becomes a light. [14]This is why it is said:

"Wake up, sleeper,

rise from the dead,

and Christ will shine on you."

Ephesians 5:15 – 21

[15]Be very careful, then, how you live—not as unwise but as wise, [16]making the most of every opportunity, because the days are evil. [17]Therefore do not be foolish, but understand what the Lord's will is. [18]Do not get drunk on wine, which leads to debauchery. Instead, be filled with the Spirit, [19]speaking to one another with psalms, hymns, and songs from the Spirit. Sing and make music from your heart to the Lord, [20]always giving thanks to God the Father for everything, in the name of our Lord Jesus Christ.

[21]Submit to one another out of reverence for Christ.

Ephesians 5:22 – 33

[22]Wives, submit yourselves to your own husbands as you do to the Lord. [23]For the husband is the head of the wife as Christ is the head of the church, his body, of which he is the Savior. [24]Now as the church submits to Christ, so also wives should submit to their husbands in everything.

[25] Husbands, love your wives, just as Christ loved the church and gave himself up for her [26]to make her holy, cleansing her by the washing with water through the word, [27]and to present her to himself as a radiant church, without stain or wrinkle or any other blemish, but holy and blameless. [28]In this same way, husbands ought to love their wives as their own bodies. He who loves his wife loves himself. [29]After all, no one ever hated their own body, but they feed and care for their body, just as Christ does the church—[30]for we are members of his body. [31]"For this reason a man will leave his father and mother and be united to his wife, and the two will become one flesh." [32]This is a profound mystery—but I am talking about Christ and the church. [33]However, each one of you also must love his wife as he loves himself, and the wife must respect her husband.

Ephesians 6:1 – 9

[1]Children, obey your parents in the Lord, for this is right. [2]"Honor your father and mother"—which is the first commandment with a promise—[3]"so that it may go well with you and that you may enjoy long life on the earth."

[4]Fathers, do not exasperate your children; instead, bring them up in the training and instruction of the Lord.

[5]Slaves, obey your earthly masters with respect and fear, and with sincerity of heart, just as you would obey Christ. [6]Obey them not only to win their favor when their eye is on you, but as slaves of Christ, doing the will of God from your heart. [7]Serve wholeheartedly, as if you were serving the Lord, not people, [8]because you know that the Lord will reward each one for whatever good they do, whether they are slave or free.

[9]And masters, treat your slaves in the same way. Do not threaten them, since you know that he who is both their Master and yours is in heaven, and there is no favoritism with him.

Ephesians 6:10 – 16

[10]Finally, be strong in the Lord and in his mighty power. [11]Put on the full armor of God so that you can take your stand against the devil's schemes. [12]For our struggle is not against flesh and blood, but against the rulers, against the authorities, against the powers of this dark world and against the spiritual forces of evil in the heavenly realms. [13]Therefore put on the full armor of God, so that when the day of evil comes, you may be able to stand your ground, and after you have done everything, to stand. [14]Stand firm then, with the belt of truth buckled around your waist, with the breastplate of righteousness in place, [15]and with your feet fitted with the readiness that comes from the gospel of peace. [16]In addition to all this, take up the shield of faith, with which you can extinguish all the flaming arrows of the evil one.

Ephesians 6:17 – 20

[17]Take the helmet of salvation and the sword of the Spirit, which is the word of God.

[18]And pray in the Spirit on all occasions with all kinds of prayers and requests. With this in mind, be alert and always keep on praying for all the Lord's people. [19]Pray also for me, that whenever I speak, words may be given me so that I will fearlessly make known the mystery of the gospel, [20]for which I am an ambassador in chains. Pray that I may declare it fearlessly, as I should.